CIDER VINEGAR

Published and Distributed by
BENEDICT LUST PUBLICATIONS
Box 404 • New York 10156

Companion Book to CRUDE BLACK MOLASSES

Dr. Lust Speaking...

CIDER VINEGAR

*Nature's Great Health-Promoter
and Safest Cure of Obesity*

CYRIL SCOTT
and
JOHN LUST,
Naturopath

BENEDICT LUST PUBLICATIONS

Cider Vinegar
ISBN 0-87904-011-4
PRINTING HISTORY
Continuously published since the first
Beneficial Book Edition / May 1984

PUBLISHER'S NOTE: *Where any condition has progressed to a serious stage, or if uncertainty exists as to the seriousness, it is best not to delay timely professional services of a competent physician. This book may not be used in any manner to promote the sale of any products mentioned herein.*

This *Beneficial Book* edition includes every word contained in the original
edition of *Cider Vinegar*. It has been completely reset in a type
face designed for easy reading, and was printed from new plates.
Beneficial Books are published in pocket book form by a division of
Benedict Lust Publications, Box 404 Murray Hill,
New York, NY 10156 U.S.A.

Dedication

To Doctor D. C. Jarvis, the doctor who was a teacher as well as a physician.

Contents

8

WARNING

genuine Apple Cider Vinegar must be taken according to the directions. Brands such as Sterling Cider Vinegar, P.O. Box 518 Sterling, MA 01564 available in health food stores, and Heinz Apple Cider Vinegar are suitable because they are made from whole cider apples. (As I have no financial interest in Apple Cider Vinegar, this warning is entirely unbiassed.)

CYRIL SCOTT.

Dr. Lust Speaking...

ABOUT APPLE CIDER VINEGAR AND YOU

Your metabolism, the exchange of matter within your body governs whether you are overweight or underweight. Normally it also produces the interferon that immunizes you naturally against killer diseases.

Dr. Jarvis states that potassium in its natural combination with other trace minerals is so essential to the metabolic process in every form of life on earth that without it there would be no life. He told a story about how his Vermont neighbors checked the rate of their own body growth and repair as an indicator of their potassium levels. Assuming that it takes five months to grow a new thumbnail and ten months to grow a new nail for the big toe, they would make a mark with a nail file at the base of the thumbnail and of the toenail. The date was then recorded on a calendar. At the end of five months, if growth was normal, the mark on the thumbnail would be at the top edge—at ten months the mark on the toenail at the outer edge of that nail. If the file mark reached either point before or after the expected date, it indicated whether one's growth rate was faster or slower than normal. If less, it indicated to them a lack of potassium foods in their diets.

One of the functions of potassium in your system

is to keep the tissues soft and pliable. Potassium is to the soft tissues what calcium is to the hard tissues, the skeleton. Hardening of the arteries takes place more readily in the presence of a potassium-poor blood chemistry.

What has all that to do with apple cider vinegar? Simply this, your life process, your metabolism, requires a balanced intake of vitamins, minerals and enzymes.

Apple cider vinegar is an excellent source of all those including the key mineral, potassium. Potassium is never found in its pure state in nature, but always in association with other elements. Thus it is reasonable to conclude that potassium in its crude natural form provides traces of nutrition in a combined formula that is compatible with your needs. Using synthetic pure drugs produces a far more potent substance that is also far more capable of serious side effects—even death if one's elimination is poor or kidney function is impaired.

To insure a healthful potassium level in your bloodstream include in your daily diet fresh fruit or unsulphured dried fruits, apricots, raisins, prunes, cherries, berries, grapes, bananas, watermelon, leafy vegetables, root vegetables, garlic, parsley, watercress, potatoes (with the skin), squash, parsnips, honey, molasses, and apple cider beverage.

This diet reform, selecting from the above list and avoiding red meat, is especially necessary when diuretics are being used daily to reduce high blood pressure or for any other reason. The increased urination drains your potassium level.

It's a fact that apple cider vinegar has been noted to affect the body's acid-alkaline balance as an alkaline food. The organic acids are oxidized in the body to furnish energy and leave an alkaline base residue in the blood. The rich source of alkaline-forming elements, potassium, calcium, magnesium, phosphorous, chlorine, sodium, sulphur, iron, fluorine, silicon, plus many trace minerals in the apple leads to a formation of urine that is less acid. The apple safeguards the body against acidosis and its attendant ailments such as indigestion, gout, ulcers, gas and bloating. These properties are not lost in apple cider vinegar.

Many theories have been advanced as to why cider vinegar works. It may be that there is not one specific answer, but several. Research has been undertaken in connection with obesity and asthma, two very prevalent disorders that have enjoyed excellent results from this folk remedy.

It is helpful to know another researcher found that the malic acid content of apples dissolves calcium deposits, and that the alkaline residue left by this acid-rich vinegar in its buffering function, aids in recovery from colds, flu, virus infections, and hangovers. The acid in apple cider vinegar has also been credited with cures for those afflicted with arthritis, rheumatism and kidney stones.

Clearly, it is encouraging to experiment with this folk remedy. I had a report from one woman who a year ago started taking the apple cider beverage as described in this book. Her problem—she weighed 250 pounds. She said she had lost 50 pounds and was satisfied to stay with it for another year.

As a note of caution, where any condition has progressed to a serious stage, or if uncertainty exists as to the seriousness, it is best not to delay timely professional services of a competent physician. Naturopaths, many Chiropractors and even Medical doctors are now trained to utilize nutrition as a curative aid.

INTRODUCTION

Some impressive articles by Dr. D. C. Jarvis, M.D., of Barre, Vermont, drew attention to the highly valuable properties contained in Cider Vinegar. In fact, the number of ailments which will automatically disappear after taking Cider Vinegar in the prescribed manner is so astonishing that I feel a book should be written on the subject similar to the one I wrote on Crude Black Molasses. This latter, by way of emphasis, I called a "natural Wonder food," and in view of the evidence collected, Cider Vinegar may justly be called a "natural Wonder beverage." But it must be noted at the outset that no other type of vinegar will produce the same therapeutic effects, though the vinegar made from wine which the Italians take is to some extent a substitute.

Dr. Jarvis first came to appreciate the curative value of Cider Vinegar through his contact with Rural Medicine, as practiced for some three hundred years in Vermont, and as evolved by the trial and error method until it reached its high state of efficiency about which Dr. Jarvis, with considerable broadmindedness and courage, speaks in no mean terms. For undoubtedly it shows courage for a doctor with orthodox qualifications to expound the rationale of what many of his less broadminded colleagues might well dismiss as nothing but "old wives tales." Moreover, when doctors express themselves in print, it is usually to draw learned attention to some new drug or treatment, and not to a simple aliment which can be bought in most countries at any grocers. Therefore all honor to Dr. Jarvis. A tribute which the reader will come to think is fully justified when he has read these pages and come to appreciate what a polychrest (that which cures various diseases) Cider Vinegar has proved to be.

Meanwhile it may be asked why this common table fluid should be so beneficial? And the very simple and self-evident answer is that it is made from apples, which are perhaps the most health-giving fruits that exist. "An apple a day keeps the doctor away" is no empty slogan, for apples contain some very important chemical ingredients.* A second question may run; what are the functions of Cider Vinegar; or in vulgar parlance, exactly what does it do? Well, stated in brief, it does a variety of things, on which we shall enlarge anon. It favours oxidation of the blood; it tends to prevent intestinal putrefaction; it regulates calcium metabolism; it retards the onset of old age; it renders the urine normal, thus counteracting the too frequent urge to urinate; it affects the blood, making it of the right consistency; it regulates menstruation, and hence is very beneficial for women; it cures and prevents obesity; it promotes digestion, for the reason that Cider Vinegar bears a closer resemblance to the digestive juices than does any other liquid. . . . And so, taking all in all, though it may not be a universal panacea, it is a polychrest of such extensive range if taken in the manner hereafter to be indicated, that, fearing to overtax cre-

NOTE: The writer cannot guarantee that pasteurized brands of Cider Vinegar are as remedially effective as the unpasteurized type.

dulity, I would hesitate to place the facts before the public, were it not for the following considerations: (1) the most gratifying reception given to my book on Molasses, (2) that people who take an intelligent interest in matters of health are more and more coming to the conclusion that disease is a unity, and hence that a number of apparently disconnected diseases have but one prime cause.

OBESITY

It is, generally speaking, safe to say that obesity is a condition which has somewhat puzzled the medical profession for many years; for although numerous theories about it exist, they do not entirely solve the whole problem. The simple explanation that corpulence is merely due to overeating does not cover all the facts. If greed were the sole cause of it, how can one account for the well-known case of Daniel Lambert, who was only a moderate eater and drank nothing but water, yet his enormous weight amounted to 739 pounds? Granted I am here citing a very extreme case; but there have been less extreme ones which are correspondingly inexplicable—not to overlook the fact that living today are thousands of grossly overweight people of both sexes, despite their being very small eaters.

In this connection the maxim holds good that whereas there may be many truths about this or that, there are certain puzzling things for which the real truth can only be ascertained when several branches of knowledge are brought into alignment. This book is concerned with one of those branches.

To state the circumstances: several decades ago, a few impressive articles appeared in *The Medical World* of U.S.A. by a leading authority in Vermont folk medicine, in which he drew attention to the highly valuable properties contained in Cider Vinegar; a fact generally unknown or ignored, save by the votaries of this folk medicine, as practiced for some three hundred years and evolved by the trial and error method until it reached its present state of efficiency. Therefore, that it and its achievements might be more widely recognized, was the reason which prompted me to present the evidence with its resultant benefits, in the following pages.

As so many women are assailed with the fear of getting fat, I will deal with this condition first, though it is not looked upon as a disease in the ordinary use of the word. All the same, as the tendency to put on too much flesh occurs with either sex, it shows that "something is wrong somewhere," though exactly what, orthodox medicos seem unable to state. When excessive corpulence is exhibited in the case of young persons, it is often attributed to defective action of some of the endocrine glands; and this may be correct. The assumption may also prove correct in the case of much older persons; but why the action of these glands is defective we are not told. That obesity often eventuates from the habit of imbibing too many alcoholic liquors, most of us have observed, but in that case the reason is obviously that the tissues get full of fluid, as the bloated appearance of the face suggests. Further, there are certain drugs which are apt to cause obesity, and it has been noticed that persons who for some reason have been taking mercury or arsenic over a long period tend to increase in bulk. But leaving aside such obvious causes as over-eating, a sendentary life, and a lack of fresh air, as also the over-consumption of starchy and sugary foods, the prime cause of obesity is the insufficient oxidation of the blood. Yet not realizing this fact, women (in particular) will often resort to slimming measures and advertised slimming drugs which may prove very harmful in the end. Now the safe and salubrious treatment, proved over years of trial, is to be found in nothing more complicated than Cider Vinegar; the reason being, as already implied, that the aliment is conducive to the proper oxidation of the blood.

The *modus operandi* is as follows: Two teaspoonsful of the Cider Vinegar in a tumbler of water to be taken on rising in the morning. To get the desired effect, the practice is to be continued over a long period. Obesity cannot be expected to vanish in twenty-four hours, nor is it desirable that it should, as the skin requires ample time to re-adjust itself.

In severe cases Cider Vinegar can be taken as above indicated with the chief meals of the day, as well as in the morning. The beverage should be sipped so that the whole contents of the glass have been exhausted when the meal is finished. This, in addition to its other effects, modifies the desire to over-eat, and also promotes digestion.

Dr. Jarvis has kindly furnished me with the following two case histories, though many more could be selected from his own casebook, and from the archives of Vermont Folk Medicine:—(See Apendix)

(1) Patient, 31 years old. When she started the treatment she weighed 148 lbs. Most of her bulk was in the posterior, and she had developed what in U.S.A. is called "stenographer's seat." By dint of taking the diluted Cider Vinegar every morning before breakfast (not at any other times) she gradually lost her excessive weight, and her so-termed stenographer's seat completely disappeared. Nevertheless she continues to take the beverage every morning, with the gratifying result that she can eat what she

likes and to the amount her appetite demands without putting on weight.

(2) Patient aged 50. She had to give up work owing to bad heart. In 1945 she weighed 208 lbs. She then started taking the Cider Vinegar beverage with her meals, and by 1947 had reduced her weight to 164 lbs., although she had made no alteration in her diet. As she lost weight her heart condition materially improved.

Dr. Jarvis mentions other cases in which the Cider Vinegar beverage was taken from one to three times a day, during or not during meals, the result being a gradual reduction of weight, which remained a permanent one. No change of diet was made in any of these cases; the Cider Vinegar beverage by itself having enabled these sufferers to burn up their surplus fat.

According to Vermont Folk Medicine: if a woman who is too stout will take one teaspoonful of Cider Vinegar in a glass of water during meals, she will generally observe that in two months her waistline has been reduced one inch. In four months two inches, and so on. But a noteworthy fact is that reduction in bulk is by no means always associated with reduction of weight. Where comparatively young women are concerned, though the tape measure may show a loss of fat, the scales will often show an actual increase in weight; the reason being an increased deposit of calcium in the bone-framework of the body due to the improved metabolism. And that the latter *has* improved is evidenced from a marked decrease in dental decay. It seems needless to add that under the Cider Vinegar treatment, surplus fat will gardually disappear no matter where it is present, and whether it takes the form of a double chin or an accentuated bosom. Incidentally, in Vermont Folk Medicine one finds the following description of a perfectly proportioned woman: viz., twice around the wrist should equal once around the neck; twice around the neck (at its lowest part) should equal once around the waist. When these proportions are not present, then it is considered that there is insufficient burning up of surplus fat, and that the individual cannot be termed in perfect health.

Of course most of us are aware that vinegar has been used as a slimming agent for a great many years (there was a time when Byron lived on vinegar and biscuits because he was getting too stout), but what should be stressed is that ordinary vinegar must *not* be used, as it does not contain the properties of vinegar made from apples, and in the long run would certainly prove harmful. We must remember, however much we may blink our eyes to the fact, that stoutness is really a disorder which we recognize in the domestic animal kingdom but disregard in the human unless pronounced enough to be unsightly. Therefore, being a disorder, the only safe and rational way of combating it lies in a method that is conducive to better metabolism and hence improved health. All the evidence goes to show that the Cider Vinegar treatment will achieve this object.

EFFECTS OF CIDER VINEGAR ON THE BLOOD

When the blood is out of order owing to a deficiency of the required mineral salts and vitamins, all kinds of diseases from boils and rheumatism to cancer may occur according to the make-up of the individual. This everyone knows who has studied even the rudiments of therapeutics. There is a condition, however, which has baffled most therapeuticians, and persons suffering from this order are called "Bleeders," the general verdict being that nothing can be done for them, consequently they live in dread of the most trifling accident such as the cutting of a finger or a mishap while shaving.

Now it is an impressive fact that the taking of Cider Vinegar in the manner already indicated, favors that clotting of the blood which fails to occur in the case of Bleeders. The reason is again to be found in the improved metabolism which the vinegar brings about. Exponents of that most effective Therapy known as The Biochemic System of Medicine, maintain that Haemophilia (as it is called), occurs when there is a deficiency of phosphate of potash, phosphate of iron, and to some extent chloride of sodium in the blood. Thus Cider Vinegar favors the assimilation of these salts, especially if two teaspoonful of honey are added to the beverage. (I will

deal with this later.) Meanwhile we will consider
the use of Cider Vinegar respecting surgical operations.

CIDER VINEGAR AS A HEALING AGENT

According to Vermont Folk Medicine, if an operation is necessary following some accident, the healing process can be greatly quickened by directing the patient to take one or more teaspoonsful of Cider Vinegar in half or a whole glass of water with each meal. This practice should be continued for two or more weeks. If desired, the patient can drink the beverage between meals instead. All the evidence goes to show the astonishing efficacy of this simple treatment.

Bleeding can be reduced to a minimum by the same expedient in the case, say, of an operation on the nose for adenoids or polyps, and at the same time all likelihood of post-operative haemorrhage can be prevented. Where patients have contrived to take the Cider Vinegar treatment for a whole month before the operation, it has been found that the bleeding hardly amounts to a dozen drops. (I should, however, add in parenthesis that as both adenoids and polyps indicate a lack of certain mineral salts, operations can be avoided in many cases if these are taken. Furthermore that as the habitual taking of Cider Vinegar improves the metabolism of the body, operations are rarer occurrences in Vermont than in most countries where the Medical Profession resorts to surgery almost on the slightest pretext.)

MENSTRUATION

The number of women who suffer during their periods is legion. If menstruation is too profuse, then the Cider Vinegar treatment will reduce the flow to about fifty per cent, that is to say to normality. Moreover the amount of clots will be greatly decreased. This may sound like a contradiction to what has already been stated regarding the power of Cider Vinegar to cause blood coagulation; but therein lies the "magic" of this health giving liquid—its action normalizes abnormalities. For instance, there are certain naturopathic treatments which cause some people who are too thin to become stouter, and other people who are too stout to become thinner; and if one wonders why there should be this paradoxical action, the simple answer is that such treatments promote health and consequently normality. In the case of menstruation, I should add here that (as Dr. Jarvis points out) before normality is established, the vinegar treatment may in some cases delay the onset of menstruation for a few days. Should this occur, it is advisable to cease taking the beverage for three or four days prior to the expected menstrual date. The Cider Vinegar treatment can then be continued when menstruation has set in.

HEMORRHAGES, CUTS, WOUNDS, ETC.

Vermonters say in colloquial parlance that Cider Vinegar "dries up the blood." This is of course an overstatement. What they really mean is that as soon as a man cuts himself while shaving or in any other way, the blood clots immediately on coming into contact with the air, and there is practically no bleeding. This observation having been made years ago, in cases where wounds do not heal as quickly as they should, the following procedure is resorted to: Two teaspoonsful of Cider Vinegar are taken in half or a whole glass of water both at meals and between meals, making six glasses in all. A weak solution of the vinegar is also applied to the wound itself. The result is, Dr. Jarvis declares, a rapid healing.

In cases of frequent nose-bleeding due to some indeterminate cause, a drink of the vinegar beverage with each meal will soon put a stop to the trouble.

The same treatment is prescribed for any indefinite hemorrhage of a small amount, from either the respiratory or the gastro-intestinal tract, so as to prevent the liability to further hemorrhage until the cause of the bleeding has been discovered. This power to stop hemorrhage again serves to demonstrate the pronounced effect Cider Vinegar has on the body processes; and Dr. Jarvis acknowledges all he owes to Vermont Folk Medicine where the treatment of the sick is concerned.

EFFECT OF CIDER VINEGAR ON THE EYES

With the creeping on of old age, or even earlier, many people find themselves unable to read for any length of time with comfort, or they discover that they have grown sensitive to strong light, such as that of a sunny day. When these discomforts appear, most people, under the assumption that their eyes are "wearing out," go to the occulist, who generally prescribes stronger glasses; or if cataract is observed, then an operation, despite the fact that the latter only tinkers with an effect, but does not remove the cause of the trouble. The reason is that most eye troubles are the result of defective metabolism, and merely to treat them locally is neither reasonable nor scientific. For instance cataract develops where there is a deficiency of fluoride of calcium, phosphate of potash and silica in the body; this is another fact we have learned from therapeutic biochemistry. I am not here implying that Cider Vinegar is a specific for cataract, but I am implying that where perfect metabolism is present, it is many chances to one that this distressing condition will not occur. As dogs are said to develop cataract if constantly lying in front of a hot fire, it may be that humans who have to be frequently near a furnace may develop it likewise. But here we are mentioning unusual circumstances.

What I would point out is that with normally occupied persons, the Cider Vinegar treatment will improve vision owing to the improvement in metabolism it brings about. Thus, Vermonters who practice Folk Medicine maintain that if there is sensitiveness to light, or discomfort while reading, the Cider Vinegar beverage, taken with each meal, will usually get rid of these troubles within from one to two months; for the treatment creates "within the body a new biochemical background," so making it possible for the vitamin A effect to become operative. The good effects of the beverage, however, are enhanced if two teaspoonsful of honey are added to the mixture, as honey not only contains many of the vitamins, but also a number of the needed mineral salts, among them potassium and silica. I will enlarge on this vinegar and honey combination later on.

IMPAIRED HEARING

When this is not due to some serious trouble, the same treatment as above is indicated. Apropos of deafness, it is a deplorable thing that orthodox doctors should still dose patients suffering from malaria with repeated doses of quinine, considering that the biochemic tissue-salt natrum sulph. is a much safer remedy, and does not cause deafness like quinine. Should the latter have been given, then natrum mur. 6x should be taken for a period, before any improvement in hearing can be expected.

EAR DISCHARGE

The method of treating ear-discharge when it occurs during one of the childhood diseases is as follows: One teaspoonful of Cider Vinegar in a glass of water, to be taken in the middle of the morning and again in the middle of the afternoon. Under this simple treatment the discharge disappears quickly. It is amusing to note that when Dr. Jarvis—so he relates—first settled in Vermont, he was quite at a loss to understand why persons well grounded in Vermont Folk Medicine should think that an ear disease could possibly be cured by treating it in this manner via the mouth. But later on when he came to employ the same method himself, he found how efficacious it always proved. In orthodox medical practice it would almost seem as if doctors and specialists were oblivious of the fact that the ear is a part of the human body, and not an organ detached from the physical vehicle of consciousness. Otorrhoea can only eventuate where there is a deficiency of certain of the mineral salts. Which ones are particularly lacking can be ascertained from the color and nature of the discharge itself. In short, once again the matter boils down to defective metabolism, and that is why the above mentioned treatment produces a speedy cure.

NOSE TREATMENT

Our druggists sell all sorts of nostrums for what we call "a stuffy nose," yet according to Vermont Folk Medicine nothing is so effective (and so cheap) as Cider Vinegar used as an inhalant. In a suitable vessel the vinegar is placed so as to reach a depth of about 2 inches. The vessel is then placed on a stove until its contents begin to steam. The vapor is then inhaled. Thereafter the nasal passages will remain clear from 12 to 24 hours. If necessary the inhalation is repeated. The effects of this treatment are to remove the congestion, to allay the inflammation of the mucous membrane, and to kill the cold-germs. Should the vinegar inhalation be too strong to be tolerated, then a little water can be added. The Cider Vinegar beverage should be taken with meals, or when convenient, to speed up the cure. Dr. Jarvis maintains, by the way, that this special kind of vinegar has an adrenalin-like effect; hence its power to stop bleeding.

SORE THROAT

All the evidence goes to show that sore throat, even of the streptococcus type, can be cured with astonishing rapidity—often in one day—by using

Cider Vinegar as a gargle. The fashionable drugs "cannot approach," writes Dr. Jarvis, "the sureness and swiftness of the result obtained with the cider vinegar gargle." Moreover the indiscriminate use of antibiotics may have very undesirable effects, as I, personally, have seen in many cases. The Cider Vinegar treatment consists of adding one teaspoonful of the vinegar to a glass of water. Every hour the sufferer should gargle with one mouthful of the mixture. A second mouthful should then be taken, gargled with, and then swallowed. This procedure should be repeated every sixty minutes during waking hours, or even in the night if the patient cannot sleep. As soon as the soreness has improved, the intervals of gargling, etc., can be lengthened to two hours. When the patient is cured it is advisable to use the gargle after each meal for a few days to insure that there will be no return of the trouble.

TICKLING COUGH

Towards the end of a cold, many people suffer from that annoying and sleep-preventing irritation we call a "tickling cough." In many cases neither lozenges nor other measures have any result. As to most cough-mixtures which doctors prescribe, they contain a drug to deaden the nerve, and drugs in the long run are harmful; on the other hand the Cider Vinegar treatment is both harmless and effective. All that is necessary is to place by the bedside a glass of water to which either one or two teaspoonsful of the vinegar have been added. As the tickling sensation is felt, take a few swallows of the mixture, after which the "tickle" will rapidly disappear, leaving the sufferer able to sleep again.

ACUTE LARYNGITIS

For this distressing condition the effect of the Cider Vinegar treatment is almost miraculous. The dosage is one teaspoonful of the vinegar to half a glass of water, the mixture to be taken every hour for seven hours. In most cases the sufferer will be talking normally again after the seventh dose. This treatment is also a great value as a precautionary measure when obliged to be with people suffering from the complaint.

ASTHMA

A somewhat similar treatment is very helpful in cases of that mild type of asthma which only occurs during the night, and where the wheezing interferes with sleep. One tablespoonful of Cider Vinegar is added to a tumbler of water, which should be taken in sips for half an hour. The patient should then wait half an hour, then the procedure should be repeated. If the wheezing should still persist, though usually it has gone by then, a second glass of the same mixture should be sipped.

Sufferers from severe forms of asthma would be well advised to consult a naturopathic or a biochemic practitioner, as few orthodox doctors are successful in dealing with this distressing complaint. Quite often it occurs as the result of suppressing some skin disease. The homœopath, being aware of this fact, will therefore treat it accordingly. Very important are breathing exercises. Deep breathing should be practised gradually, and if persisted with every day, will, in combination with the Cider Vinegar treatment, most likely effect a cure, especially if the cause of the disorder has first been ascertained and dealt with by a competent practitioner.

THE MIND. MENTAL VIGOR IN OLD AGE

There are two methods by which ageing Vermont natives combat senility and loss of mental vigor. One is the habitual taking of the Cider Vinegar as a beverage, the other is to take at least two glasses of cider proper every day. But unfortunately much of the cider in this country, nowadays, lacks the qualities of the Vermont kind, hence it is better to drink the Cider Vinegar beverage, which not only contains all the curative elements, but also comes much cheaper. That it has the power to retard the disabilities of old age is evidenced by the extraordinary physical and mental vigor of Vermont natives who have reached their eighties. Yet although this may be surprising on the surface, it becomes less so when we remember that Cider Vinegar favors the proper metabolism of the body. Nor is this all; for it has been found that the diluted vinegar beverage will restore mental and physical vigor in cases where it has already been lost. (I am here, of course, alluding to persons who newly resort to the treatment, and not to those who have made it a part of their daily lives.) And when I speak of mental vigor, it includes a marked improvement of the memory. Observers have been quite astonished to see how forgetfulness in old people partially or wholly disappeared after resorting to the practice of taking 1 teaspoonful of the Cider Vinegar in a whole glass of water, either with meals or between meals, whichever method is preferred or suits the individual best. I mention this because some people are apt to say that drinking with meals gives them indigestion. Precisely; if by drinking is meant gulping down large draughts of liquid. But then all liquids possessing any taste should be sipped and not imbibed in that unwise manner. If the Cider Vinegar is taken with meals in the prescribed manner, it will seldom cause indigestion, for the reason already mentioned that it bears a closer resemblance to the gastric juices than does any other fluid.

THE DIGESTIVE TRACT

Which brings us to the subject of digestion and indigestion. Many people are aware that an apple is good for biliousness; it is also the remedy to take when nausea occurs after the smoking of a too strong cigar or pipe. Therefore it is no matter of surprise that vinegar made from apples is very helpful towards the cure of many digestive troubles if taken as already indicated.

FOOD POISONING

One of the most serious, if temporary, disturbances of the digestive tract is caused, as we all know, by food poisoning. In Vermont Folk Medicine the method to cure these effects is quite simple. The sufferer adds 1 teaspoonful of Cider Vinegar to a glass of water, and sips 1-2 teaspoonsful of the mixture every 5 minutes. This procedure is repeated as many times as may be necessary. The whole contents of the glass is not taken at once, because the stomach, owing to its disordered state will not tolerate it; only in small amounts can the mixture be kept down. As soon as a marked improvement takes place, then the intervals between taking the remedy are lengthened. As the result of this treatment the painful symptoms have usually vanished within twelve hours, after which the Cider Vinegar beverage is taken with meals for a few days to complete the cure.

THE TREATMENT FOR DIARRHEA

Diarrhea being an attempt on the part of Nature to get rid of poisons in the body, only unenlightened physicians will seek to stop the attack by unnatural means, though if it continues too long, measures sometimes need to be taken to prevent it from over weakening the patient. And when I say unnatural means, I refer to such drugs as calomel or laudanum, which orthodox doctors often prescribe. Even castor oil is not good, as, like laudanum, it constipates the patient afterwards. And in any case, these drugs do not cure the cause of the disease but merely deal with its effects. Unless diarrhea is due to some serious bodily disorder, it can be cured in a very short time by the Cider Vinegar treatment; namely 1 teaspoonful of the vinegar to a glass of water, to be taken not only with meals, but in addition in the middle of the morning, in the middle of the afternoon, and again at bedtime. It does not matter what age the patient happens to be; for apart from being effective, it is so harmless that it can be given to children of only three years of age. The Cider Vinegar treatment acts as an antiseptic to the intestines and the whole digestive tract, hence it is an entirely rational method of dealing with an abnormal condition. Not only will it cure humans but also animals; a fact that has been proved over and over again. For example, when diarrea is observed in a calf, it is regarded as a very serious matter which may often end with the loss of the animal. Yet the lives of calves have been saved by giving them, via the mouth, 6 ozs. of Cider Vinegar in the same amount of water. Cows have been cured by the same simple means. Dr. Jarvis mentions the case of twenty-five cows, all of which were suffering from diarrhea at the same time, and all of which were cured; some already in one day, others in two days, and the rest by the third day. As a general tendency, after such severe attacks, there is a marked decrease in milk production, but after the Cider Vinegar treatment it was entirely normal, showing that the cows were restored to perfect health and productiveness.

CIDER VINEGAR AS AN ANTISEPTIC

I have already mentioned that the cider vinegar possesses antiseptic properties, and it may be asked what proof there is for this assertion. The answer is that after taking the Cider Vinegar beverage over a given period, there is no odor either in the flatus or in the excreta; which is enough proof in itself. The reason is that the vinegar destroys the putrefactive bacteria in the digestive tract. Let us consider another example from the animal kingdom. It has been observed that when 2 ozs. of the vinegar has been poured over the daily ration of each cow in a herd, all odor has disappeared from the excreted dung in about two months. Instead of the usual smell of cow-dung and ammonia to be sensed in most cow-sheds, there was no unpleasant smell whatsoever. But the treatment had other beneficial effects as well. If undigested hay, etc., had been observed in the excreta of cows, it was noticed that after two months there were no further indications of improper digestion. It may, of course, be objected that what applies to cows does not apply to human beings, but the facts prove this objection to be ungrounded.

To enlarge on the subject: nowadays that "a clean bowel is one of the most essential pre-requisites to good health and vigor," is a maxim the truth of which is being more and more accepted by healers of all schools. And the proof of a clean bowel is determined from the odorlessness of both flatus and excreta. Where there is odor, it nearly always means intestinal putrefaction—though admittedly offensive flatus may occur after eating raw onions, owing to the sulphur which they contain. Eggs, unless entirely fresh, are apt to produce similar unpleasant effects, likewise cabbage. But we are not concerned with the purely temporary results consequent to eating these particular aliments, but with that more or less permanent state of intestinal putrefaction which makes people an offense to others and an offense to themselves. Now in this connection it is of interest to note that putrefaction and decomposition are practically synonymous words; consequently the contentions of Dr. E. Henry Smalpage of Sydney, N.S.W., are highly significant. He maintains that *decomposition* is the prime cause of all diseases, and hence that the most rational way to prevent and cure human ills is to be found in some agent which prevents decomposition. He advocates phosphorous (though obviously in minute doses) treated in a certain way by sunlight; but as I should be accused of advertising were I to go into details, more cannot be said in this book. The point that I may mention, however, is that apples contain phosphorous. As to the preservative element in vinegar where certain foods are concerned, of this we are all aware without my stressing the obvious. But what I would *stress* is the fact that cider vinegar by its very nature and when taken repeatedly *must* to a large extent counteract decomposition in the human body, and herein lies the reason why it retards the disabilities of old age, prevents putrefaction in the bowels, and cures or prevents the onset of many diseases. Nor is this mere theory, for the evidence proves it to be an undeniable fact. In "The Medical World," U.S., of November 1946, Dr. D. C. Jarvis pointed out that if a person takes two teaspoonsful of the cider vinegar in a glassful of water with each meal, he will observe at the end of two months (or less) that his stools and flatus are quite devoid of any offensive odor.

AUTO-INTOXICATION

From the foregoing it will be inferred, and rightly so, that Cider Vinegar is the preventive *par excellence* of auto-intoxication, from which so many people suffer to varying degrees. One reason why the vinegar prevents this disease-promoting condition is to be found in its action on the liver, for it has the power of detoxicating the poisons that accumulate in that organ, and at the same time implementing their elimination from the body. Cider Vinegar may therefore aptly be called an hepatic remedy, and one namely which possesses none of those disadvantages present in many drugs which people are in the habit of taking for what they are wont to term "a touch of liver." For proper elimination, a substance called pectin is necessary, as it has the power to draw water to itself; to cause a swelling of foods "responsible for the bulk in the intestine"; it is moreover a binding, jellifying and hence a thickening agent. As pectin is an ingredient in Cider Vinegar to the former may be ascribed its capacity to promote adequate and healthy action of the bowels, similar to that produced by taking linseeds (whole) last thing at night with water. The linseeds swell and to some extent jellify, and thus produce the desired effect. But that is merely by the way; the linseed treatment will in most cases not be required if the Cider Vinegar beverage is taken. Nowadays we hear of the necessity of creating "bulk" in the intestines, but as this necessitates the eating of more than it may be advisable to consume, the cider vinegar treatment is to be preferred, seeing that it enables the appetite to be satisfied with a lesser amount of food.

BELCHING, HEARTBURN, BAD TASTE, HICCOUGHS

Unless due to some serious disorder of the stomach, or to the habit of swallowing air, belching can be cured or greatly lessened by taking the Cider Vinegar beverage with the chief meals of the day.

As for heartburn, that burning sensation which may occur after meals—sometimes one or two hours after—this often disappears entirely after resorting to the Cider Vinegar beverage or at any rate it is much lessened.

When a bad taste in the mouth is noticed on rising of a morning, one teaspoonful of the vinegar to a glassful of water if used as a mouthwash will quickly dispel it.

Hiccoughs, when not due to some serious condition, can be relieved at once by taking one teaspoonful of Cider Vinegar *neat* (Dr. Jarvis).

EFFECT OF CIDER VINEGAR ON THE URINE

If the urine is either too acid or too alkaline, that troublesome and embarrassing necessity for much too frequent urination occurs in both sexes. We are of course not here concerned with serious disorders of the urinary tract, which need special treatment, but with conditions in which the urine for no very grave reason is of an abnormal consistency. In the case of younger people it is often a too alkaline urine that necessitates frequent micturation, whereas in older people the cause may be found in the fact that the urine is too acid. But whether too acid or too alkaline, it can, according to Vermont Folk Medicine be brought back to normal if the Cider Vinegar beverage (two teaspoonsful of vinegar to the glass of water) be taken with the chief meals of the day. Elderly men will often find this treatment very helpful in relieving the frequent desire to pass urine during the night. Strange to say, this may occur, not always from drinking too much, but from drinking too little *water*; in which case the urine becomes too concentrated and so causes an irritation which provokes the constant urge to micturate. When this happens, elderly men are apt to get apprehensive and imagine they are suffering from prostate trouble, whereas the real cause may be nothing more serious than a too acid condition of their urine which the Cider Vinegar treatment will set right. ... Naturally people can inadvisedly drink too much fluid instead of too little. But here again the cider beverage proves very useful, for if taken with meals it allays any sensation of thirst between mealtimes. Yet should thirst occur owing to very hot weather, it proves to be one of the best thirst-quenchers that exists. It also has the power to allay the pangs of hunger, if for some reason a meal has to be omitted. If two teaspoonsful of honey can be added to the drink, so much the better; the combination of the two aliments has been found to be very sustaining. I shall have a few words to say about this combination later on.

TREATMENT FOR THE HAIR

At a certain time of the year it is normal for the hair to fall out when being combed, but should new hairs not grow again, and the falling-out period be unduly protracted, thus showing a pronounced thinning of the hair, it is an indication of faulty metabolism and an abnormal state which needs correction. Now repeated observation has proved that if the Cider Vinegar beverage is taken with or between meals (one teaspoon to the glass of water) not only will the hair cease to fall out, but it will grow much more rapidly and more thickly, especially if one level teaspoon of horseradish is taken with the two chief meals of the day. The desired effect will be produced in from one to two months. Falling out of the hair is primarily due to deficiency of the tissue-salts chloride of sodium (in minute doses), phosphate of calcium, and silica; sulphate of calcium may also be lacking in some cases. Thus the cider vinegar, through its remarkable properties, re-establishes the balance, supplies the deficiencies, and so effects a cure, if persisted in long enough. It is even advisable to continue the Cider Vinegar treatment indefinately to insure that there be no recurrence of the trouble.

THE FINGER NAILS

When the nails become too thin or fragile and tear, bend, peel, or break; in short, when they are not of normal thickness and strength, that is again a sign of faulty metabolism, which the Cider Vinegar treatment will remedy. Persons with defective nails have noticed that after taking the vinegar beverage over a certain time for the purpose of curing some ailment, their nails have automatically undergone a decided change for the better; in fact they have become healthy and normal again. Furthermore, if any white spots had been present, these have disappeared. All of which points to the effects of the Cider Vinegar on the mineral metabolism of the body.

THE TEETH. SORE MOUTH

Thanks to Dr. D. C. Jarvis and to Vermont Folk Medicine I have already been able to draw attention to the beneficial effects of the cider vinegar beverage on the teeth; this as briefly stated before, being due to the improved calcium metabolism which the vinegar brings about. But local measures are also indicated to prevent decay, and particularly to get rid of plaque deposit, or to prevent it from forming. For this purpose one teaspoonful of the Cider Vinegar should be added to a glass of water for a mouthwash, which should be used night and morning. The teeth should also be brushed with the solution. By this simple procedure the teeth will be whitened and be much less liable to decay. I may add that the whiteness of the Vermonters' teeth is a striking proof of the efficacy of this combined treatment of taking the Cider Vinegar beverage as a habit and of using the solution as a dentifrice. Incidentally, the lime deposit in a kettle can be easily removed by adding two tablespoonsful of the vinegar to the kettle of water, then leaving it for a time, after which the lime will come away when the water is poured out of the vessel: or it can the more easily be scraped away without injuring the interior surface.

For "canker sores" in the mouth, Vermont Folk Medicine prescribes the same solution as for the preservation of the teeth; namely one teaspoonful of the Cider Vinegar to a glass of water, the mixture to be used frequently as a mouth-wash. Under this treatment the sores will generally have vanished within twenty-four hours.

For gums that have a marked tendency to bleed, the Cider Vinegar beverage should be taken with meals, and the mouthwash used as above indicated.

TREATMENT FOR THE JOINTS

When the joints in any part of the body start to "creak," the Cider Vinegar beverage should be taken with meals. It has generally been noticed that under this treatment the cure will be effected in about one month: though in the case of a calcium deposit in the shoulder bursa, it may take two months. "Creaking joints" are apt to occur in elderly people, but according to Vermont Folk Medicine, age as a general rule proves no obstacle to the cure. Regarded from the biochemic standpoint "creakings" become noticeable where there is a deficiency of minute doses of sodium chloride in the system. This may seem curious, as most people eat salt (much too much of it): but then salt taken in crude doses as a condiment has a very different effect from the triturated kind. The human body can only absorb the mineral salts in the infinitesimal quantities in which Nature supplies them; hence, strange though it may sound, a person can be starved of salt even when he eats a large amount of it. Too much common salt disturbs the metabolism of the body, consequently it is best to cut down its consumption to a minimum, and so give the Cider Vinegar treatment every facility to do its work.

VERTIGO

Dizziness may arise from various causes, some of them serious, others transient, such as a disordered stomach or liver. Heart-trouble and anemia of the brain are often responsible for giddiness, and of course both these grave conditions require special treatment. In some cases where anemia is present or where the heart is involved, molasses often proves most useful as a heart-muscle strengthener. (See book entitled "Crude Black Molasses").* If molasses should be unobtainable, then black treacle is of value. Sufferers from "heart" should always eat honey instead of jam, owing to the valuable properties that the former contains and on which I shall enlarge later. For anemia, blackstrap molasses has proved to be remarkably curative. The crude doses of iron so often prescribed by orthodox doctors are not only apt to be useless but also harmful, whereas the iron in blackstrap molasses is assimilated by the organism and hence is frequently productive of the desired result when all other treatments have failed. Even so, the Cider Vinegar beverage can be profitably employed to enhance the treatment. Should vertigo not be associated with serious diseases the cider vinegar taken with meals will, judging from all the evidence, bring about a cure in from four to eight weeks. One may ask if there is any hope of relief or cure in cases of Méniére's disease? To which I can only reply that there is at any rate *some* hope, for the following reason. The giddiness with this disease is usually caused by hemorrhage into the internal ear; but as we have seen from the testimony supplied, the Cider Vinegar treatment both prevents and cures the tendency to internal bleeding, therefore it would be fairly reasonable to infer that in some cases good results might be obtained. Indeed for all one knows, in Vermont Folk Medicine may be found the most rational means of combating the disorder. In any event, in view of its harmlessness, it could be tried.

*Available directly from this Publisher
Benedict Lust Publications
P.O. Box 404
New York, NY 10156
($1.95 + $1.00 handling)

TWITCHINGS

There is an annoying if minor complaint which manifests itself in twitchings of the eyelid or corner of the mouth. This is occasionally noticeable in fairly young children. Dr. Jarvis reports that he cures this nervous condition by prescribing one teaspoonful of the vinegar in a glass of equal parts of grape juice and water; the mixture to be taken in the middle of the morning and again in the middle of the afternoon. Fortunately, one can easily but Grape juice in this country at the Health Food Stores. Fresh grapes themselves are not cheap. The treatment would prove rather expensive for most parents, even though it need not be continued as a general rule for more than two weeks.

NETTLE RASH

For this condition the Cider Vinegar beverage should be taken with meals until the disorder clears up. It is usually due to food poisoning resulting from eating shell-fish or the like, and as we have seen that the vinegar is a remedy for same. I need not go into further details.

ECZEMA, DANDRUFF

For this troublesome complaint the Cider Vinegar beverage should be taken with meals, and the vinegar, diluted, applied to the skin. For dandruff it should be applied to the scalp.

Eczema can occur as one of the long delayed after-effects of vaccination. In general it arises from a deficiency of chloride of potassium (kali mur.) in the organism, especially if it is of the fibrinous type, with mealy flour-like scales. And here it is worthy of note that kali mur. is one of the minerals contained in apples, hence the value of the vinegar, for this salt is not lost even though the apples forming it have undergone a transformation. The dry type of eczema is frequently the result of eating too much common salt, in which case it stands to reason that the habit should be discontinued. If people *must* take salt with their meals, then they can procure Nontoxic Biochemic Table Salt at the Health Food Stores. As this contains all the twelve tissue salts it does not upset the chemical balance of the body. To speed up recovery, attention should be paid to diet. The treatment of eczema with suppressive ointments is a gross misdemeanor against Nature, as every naturopath knows and every doctor ought to know. If poisons which are seeking a way out of the body through the skin are prevented from doing so, the result is a foregone conclusion to all persons with an ounce of intelligence. Need more be said?

EFFECTS OF SUMMER HEAT

The Cider Vinegar counteracts the fatigue and lassitude which many people feel in hot weather.

* * *

I have now given a fairly long list of the various complaints that yield to a treatment which is as simple as it is effective. Doubtless several more could be added to the list, but it seems unnecessary to do so if the reader will bear in mind that Cider Vinegar is not a specific for any given disease or diseases but a promoter of general health. This it brings about, I repeat, by its influence on the metabolism and oxidative processes of the body. When these are defective, it is noticeable from many signs to which the majority of people pay little attention, being under the impression that they are merely the unavoidable results of advancing years, and that nothing can be done about them. Yet the exponents of the Folk Medicine in question think otherwise. To sum up: they maintain that metabolism and oxidation are inadequate, and health not up to standard level when the body shows signs of growing fat whilst the hair shows signs of growing thin; when the teeth are apt to decay; when the eyes get easily tired; when hearing is impaired; when the finger nails are fragile; when the joints begin to creak, to say nothing of the onset of what are recognised as actual diseases. These manifestations need not inevitably occur, say the Vermont Folk Medicine practitioners, if the right steps are taken to prevent them. What the first and important step consists of will have become obvious to the reader; but the therapy can be enhanced by the use of honey, which is so valuable a substance, that for the benefit of those who do not appreciate the fact, I will go into some details relative to its constituents.

THE APPLE CIDER VINEGAR AND HONEY COMBINATION

Honey is not sufficiently appreciated in this country except by naturopaths and the like, despite the fact that Russian medico-scientists have shown that it will cure such a serious condition as gastric ulcer. Many English people complain that this poetic, fragrant "syrup of the bees" is far too sickly to suit the palate. Its sickliness however, soon vanishes if taken mixed with the cider vinegar in the proportions to be mentioned anon. Meanwhile in order to awaken some enthusiasm for honey in the general reader, I will mention the valuable elements it contains: though admittedly these are merely of academic interest, for the proof of the value of honey lies in its effects and not in the theories involving polysyllabic words as to why it produces those effects. To begin with, it contains Vitamin B1, called thiamine, which is to be found in the *husks* of cereal grains, and is therefore lacking in *white* bread. Secondly it contains vitamin B2, called riboflavin, which is to be found in yeast, milk, and meat, also in fish and liver. Thirdly it contains vitamin C (ascorbic acid) to be found in fresh fruits (oranges, etc.) and in fresh greenstuffs. To complete the list, honey also contains pantothenic acid, pyridoxine and nicotinic acid, the latter being part of the B2 complex. When there is a complete lack of B1 in the diet, that grave disease called beri-beri ensues, but where there is a shortage but not a complete lack of the thiamine, then muscular weakness and heart weakness are frequently the result. As for Vitamin C, a complete lack of it results in scurvy, and a partial lack of it in swellings and inflammation of the gums, loss of teeth, haemorrhages under the skin, and other serious conditions. All of which points to the fact that a well-balanced diet is the pre-requisite to health. But as in these years of disgrace it is not always possible to maintain a well-balanced diet, much the best thing to do is to take honey, seeing that it possesses all the elements essential for physical well-being. Moreover it retains those elements indefinitely, which is more than vegetables and fruits do, as unfortunately they lose some of their vitamin content within about twenty-four hours after they have been picked. The minerals in honey are even more important than the vitamins; they comprise potassium (a preventive of growths), sodium, calcium, magnesium, iron (very important), copper (good for the liver), chlorine, manganese, sulphur (the blood purifier), and silica. As these minute quantities of minerals essential for bodily health are used up in certain of the body processes, too complex to explain here, they need constantly to be replaced; hence the value of taking honey as the most simple means of achieving this end. Nor must we forget that honey also contains enzymes as they are termed, these enzymes being present in the digestive juices and in many of the tissues, consequently they aid digestion; yet honey itself requires no process of digestion before it can be utilized by the body. Nor can micro-organisms adversely affect it, for should they come into contact with it they are quickly destroyed.

In short, honey is a perfect food; it contains no harmful chemicals (or ought not to do unless it has been tampered with) and not more than one hundredth part of it is wastage. Truly it is a food for the gods.

Taking all this into consideration, two teaspoonsful of honey at the least should form part of the daily diet of ailing persons who wish to get well and of all well persons who desire to maintain their health. (I word my sentence in this somewhat curious manner, because there are numerous people, especially women, who do not wish to get well, and who for purposes of self-dramatization and the urge to evoke sympathy make as it were a hobby of ill-health. And although they enjoy the attentions of their doctors, they would be very disappointed if one or the other cured their complaints. For such professional invalids of course nothing can be done, and they must be left to dree their ane weird as the Scotlanders say). Needless to say honey can be eaten in place of jam, or strained honey can with advantage be added to the Cider Vinegar beverage, in which case it makes a very palatable drink. That eminent hydropathist, the late Father Kneipp of Germany maintained that if a little honey were added to all herbal remedies it greatly enhanced their efficacy, as it acted as a medium to promote better assimilation. Thus, the action of the cider vinegar can be improved and speeded by the same means. In addition to all the other things it accomplishes, the Cider Vinegar and honey combination is in many cases most helpful in promoting sound, healthy sleep.*

*For more information: See "Dr. Lust Speaking...ABOUT HONEY" $2.95 + $1.00 p.p. Order from Benedict Lust Publ./Box 404/New York, NY 10156

INSOMNIA

To combat this troublesome complaint, the following measures are advocated in Vermont Folk Medicine. According to Dr. Jarvis, an immediate improvement in the ability to sleep is brought about by taking at bedtime two teaspoonsful of the vinegar plus two teaspoonsful of honey in a glass of water. Another glassful of the mixture should be placed by the bedside so that it may be taken in case the sufferer should wake in the night.

Granted that the causes of insomnia are many and varied, yet this treatment is a rational one in view of the elements which both the cider vinegar and the honey contain. The prime cause of insomnia, though orthodox physicians seem still to be unaware of the fact, is to be found in a deficiency of phosphate of potash and phosphate of iron; though in some cases there may be also a deficiency of phosphate of magnesia. We all know of course that worry prevents one from sleeping, yet worry would not and need not prove unduly harmful if the phosphate of potash (kali phos), which it uses up were speedily replenished. As drug soporifics do not make good the deficiency, they do not and can not *cure* insomnia, even though they may make the sufferer sleep as long as he takes them. But as soon as he ceases to take them, he finds himself as sleepless as ever, thus proving their lack of power to effect a cure. I do not here deny their usefulness to induce sleep in cases of severe illnesses; but, then we are not here concerned with these but with insomnia as a complaint in itself. Again, despite what is said to the contrary, sleeping drugs are habit-forming, though they are sometimes useful to break a habit—namely that of not sleeping, when it **is** but a habit. Even so, if taken for more than a very short time, they only break one habit and form another. Therefore when all is said, bad sleepers would be well advised to try the harmless and beneficial Cider Vinegar and honey treatment. Should that fail in some cases, then it is advisable to take kali phos. 3x for a few days, three tablets thrice daily between meals. If sufferers notice that they get a flushed face at night as soon as they lie down or at other times, then ferrum phos. 3x or 6x is also indicated, and it should be taken inter-currently with the kali phos. in order to counteract the nervous tension responsible for some forms of insomnia.

HAY FEVER

Two teaspoonsful of the Cider Vinegar in a glass of water at each meal, and two teaspoonsful of the honey, also at each meal, whether added to the beverage or taken separately in place of jam.

VARIOUS HEART TROUBLES

Same treatment as above, but much enhanced by taking the molasses treatment as well. (See "Crude Black Molasses.")*

*Available where you bought this book, or direct from the publisher:
Benedict Lust Publications
P.O. Box 404 / New York, NY 10156
($1.95 + $1.00 handling)

COLITIS

Same as above. (Enemata with a teaspoonful or more of molasses, very helpful.)

NEURITIS

Same as above.

ARTHRITIS

The Cider Vinegar and honey treatment, and also the molasses treatment. Regarding the latter, I may cite a recent case history, remarkable for the rapidity of the cure. Lady turned 70. Complete fixation of the hip joints for three years. Knees could not be flexed. Much pain and fatigue. Injections given, but with no result. Specialist finally suggested an expensive operation, but could promise no success. Operation declined. Patient was then induced by an acquaintance to try molasses, which she contrived to obtain. After 36 doses she could walk without sticks and could kick her posterior with her heels. Had she then known of the Cider Vinegar and honey combination and could have combined the two therapies, the cure might well have proved even more rapid.

TOBACCO

Although Cider Vinegar antidotes tobacco, as do other vinegars (W. Boericke, M.D.), that is not to say that it counteracts the harmful effects of the paper and chemical additives in cigarettes.

DISEASES OF CIVILIZATION

It is well known that some primitive peoples have possessed excellent health until they adopted certain of the food and drink habits of civilization. And yet, as naturopaths and biochemists maintain and have proved, it is not only some of those unwholesome foods we habitually eat in civilized countries, but—paradoxical though it may sound—those foods we fail to eat, which cause so many of our present-day diseases; and I venture to include cancer.

Admittedly, flesh sustenance, denatured and processed fare, in other words, *refined* foods, may nourish the body and keep it alive; but more than just nourishment is required to keep it in sound health, to be conducive to longevity, and to the prevention of that undesirable condition politely referred to as overweight—a condition which has become increasingly noticeable as one walks the streets today.

Another sign that something must decidedly be wanting in our generally-assumed-to-be-civilized food habits is, of course, the enormous sale of medicaments of all varieties by which people seek to calm themselves or "buck themselves up", induce adequate bowel actions, relieve the pains of chronic ailments, counteract sleeplessness or whatever their respective trouble happens to be. All of which goes to show that the advice to include in one's daily diet an adequate proportion of natural vital foods, at any rate as far as possible, is a rational one based on sound principles.

A NOTE OF WARNING

A few words of warning are here advisable. Naturally the cider vinegar-honey-molasses trinity cannot work absolute miracles. It stands to reason that it cannot counteract evil vices, nor can it be expected to set right such ailments as require manipulative treatment. Last century Dr. Still of U.S.A. discovered that priceless boon to mankind known as Osteopathy, which requires no advertising from my modest pen. All I would remind the reader is this; that for such people who after paying due attention to the laws of health still find themselves ailing, the services of a competent naturopath, chiropractor or osteopath are indicated.

ANSWERS TO QUESTIONERS AND SCEPTICS

It may be asked; will Cider Vinegar suit *everybody*? And yet "everybody" is such an all-embracing word that, as the Germans say, therewith is nothing to be commenced! For instance, I know a man to whom fish is a virulent poison, and even if he merely licks a postage stamp, owing to the fish-glue, his face swells up to such an extent that he cannot see out of his eyes: yet in other respects he suffers from no ill-health. I know a woman who could not take a drink of pure water without ejecting it immediately. My own mother had an aversion to fresh fruit but could eat dried fruits with enjoyment. Many people cannot eat raw or even cooked greenstuffs without becoming painfully distended. The late Sir Arbuthnot Lane declared that most elderly people could not digest pastry—perhaps merely because he could not digest it himself. As against that, legions of persons, as we all know, can eat fish, drink water, eat both greenstuffs and pastry without suffering any untoward results. In short, there are many things that will suit many people but there is nothing that will suit *everybody*. Nevertheless it is safe to say that persons who suffer from strange indiosyncrasies are a minority and exceptions to the general rule; and if in advocating some treatment or regime one had to take all the exceptions into account, one could never advocate any treatment at all. The point is will it suit the majority, not will it suit every man, woman and child on the whole surface of the globe. As to cider vinegar, this judging from what Dr. Jarvis writes, would seem to be a natural fluid for which even young children crave. He remarks that more mothers find it necessary to hide the vinegar bottle than the sugar bowl, for if they get the chance, children will pour out the vinegar into a dish, then having dipped bread or biscuits into it, will proceed to eat them with relish. And granted that one can have too much of a good thing, this intense liking for vinegar can only be accounted for by the presence of some instinct in those children's make-up. Moreover that this instinct is a natural one will have become obvious to the reader in view of the health-promoting elements the Cider Vinegar contains, as also what it accomplishes when taken as prescribed.

Finally, a word may be addressed to sceptics who might say that the Cider Vinegar cure for human ills is all a matter of faith; for how can anything so simple prove such a polychrest? Yet if faith were the basic cause of its efficacy, it would not work with animals. . . . For the benefit of veterinary surgeons I will add some more facts to those already mentioned.

THE EFFECTS OF CIDER VINEGAR ON DOMESTIC ANIMALS

Experiments on old cows revealed that when Cider Vinegar was added to their rations, not only was the porosity of their bones arrested owing to the calcium deposit, but in consequence they became much less brittle. Yet the results of Cider Vinegar on younger cows, namely at the time of calving, have proved even more significant. Usually, after a cow has given birth to her calf, and retains her placenta, the discharge is profuse and the affluvia overpowering. These manifestations have not occurred, however, when the cow has been given by mouth 6 ozs. of Cider Vinegar added to equal parts of water, at certain times each day as long as the placenta has been retained. Of the effects of the vinegar on cows suffering from diarrhea or imperfect digestion I have written elsewhere. The action of the treatment, however, is not confined to cows, for it works equally well in the case of goats and other animals including chickens. When goats are suffering from diarrhea, four tablespoonsful of the Cider Vinegar poured over their ration at each feeding-time will quickly cure the trouble. In the case of hens, two thirds of a cup of vinegar added to 12 quarts of their drinking water will rapidly bring the birds back to normal. As for the effects of Cider Vinegar on dogs, it so greatly improves their general condition that Dr. Jarvis was constrained to write a small booklet on the subject. All of which, and much more that could be adduced, goes to prove the potency of this natural, harmless product. Still in case it should be thought that the climate and physical characteristics of the natives of Vermont should have something to do with its efficacy where they are concerned, and that it is less suited to people living in a different environment, I may add that already most gratifying results from it have been obtained in New Zealand.

APPENDIX

ARTHRITIS. I have known some spectacular cures affected by means of Parsley Tea, made like ordinary tea but taken cold. Two cups of this taken daily at some convenient times could be taken intercurrently with the Cider Vinegar treatment.

HIGH BLOOD PRESSURE. The remedy (sold at some Health Food Stores) for this affliction is "Rutin", the less expensive is Cider Vinegar, and the remedy that cost nothing at all save the trouble of picking them, is ordinary stinging nettles taken in the form of tea. A combination of the latter with the Cider Vinegar treatment is well worth considering. The two remedies to be taken intercurrently, not the one mixed with the other.

LINIMENT TO RELIEVE LAMENESS

Beat up yolk of one egg with one tablespoonful of turpentine and one tablespoonful of apple cider vinegar. Apply this to the skin surface, rubbing well in, to relieve lameness.

POISON IVY

Use equal parts of apple cider vinegar and water. Dab on the affected part and allow to dry on the skin. Apply often.

SHINGLES

Apply apple cider vinegar, just as it comes from the bottle, to the skin area where the shingles are located, four times during the day and three times during the night if you are awake. The itching and burning sensation in the skin will leave in a few minutes after the vinegar is applied, and the shingles will heal more readily with this treatment.

NIGHT SWEATS

If the skin surface of the body is given a cupped-palm hand bath of apple cider vinegar at bedtime, the night sweats will be prevented.

BURNS

Undiluted apple cider vinegar, just as it comes from the bottle, if applied to a burn on the surface of the body, will remove all smarting and soreness.

TO SHRINK VARICOSE VEINS

This is not only a remedy of Vermont Folk Medicine but, I learn from patients, is also a remedy of folk medicine in Scotland, England, and Germany. Apply apple cider vinegar, just as it comes from the bottle, to the varicose veins night and morning, by means of the cupped-hands treatment. Shrinking of the veins will be noticed at the end of the month. In addition to applying the vinegar to the veins, two teaspoonfuls of vinegar in a glass of water are taken twice a day.

IMPETIGO

Undoubtedly, impetigo is the "catchingest" disease in the world. It may be caught from one touch of a finger or one dab of a towel. Usually it begins as a red or pimply spot no bigger than a split pea. Often it appears on the cheek or around the nose, where it may be mistaken for a cold sore. Soon it begins to enlarge, blister, discharge, and spread to other parts of the body. Finally the blistery eruption dries into a yellow crust that is loosely attached.

Technically, impetigo is a staphylococcus or streptococcus infection of the skin. Anybody of any age may catch it, but children seem to be especially susceptible. Indeed, unless a patient strictly keeps his hands off his sores, he may have crop after crop, indefinitely. If, however, he controls himself, he may be well and presentable in two weeks.

In treating impetigo, use apple cider vinegar just as it comes from the bottle. Dip the finger in it and apply to each affected part of the skin. Application should be six times a day, beginning on rising in the morning and at intervals to bedtime. As a rule the impetigo will have disappeared in two to four days.

RINGWORM

For some years ringworm of the scalp has been spreading over the United States. Most commonly, the ringworm areas are rounded, scaly patches, small in size, which appear at first glance to be bald patches. Close inspection, however, will reveal hair shafts broken off close to the scalp. The ringworm patches may or may not show local inflammation. When inflammation is present, it may vary from a mild low-grade inflammation, with usually a few crusts present, through all the stages up to a marked redness, with some swelling of tissue and pus points.

Glands not far from the ringworm may be enlarged. The patches of ringworm may be single or multiple. They are most frequent on or above the back of the head, but they can appear wherever the hair is growing. Though spontaneous cures are sometimes seen, the majority of lesions tend to persist indefinitely if left untreated.

Boys are affected six to nine times more often than girls. Ringworm is due to a fungus which is transmitted directly from child to child. It may also be transmitted to children from cats and dogs. The spread of ringworm seems to be largely by way of swapped hats and caps or high-backed seats in theaters and conveyances, where children's heads can rub against the upholstery.

Apply apple cider vinegar with the fingers to the ringworm area six times a day, beginning on rising in the morning and continuing through to bedtime. Apple cider vinegar is an excellent antiseptic.

TREATMENT FOR HANGOVER

During the passing years, Vermont Folk Medicine has learned by the trial and error method how to deal successfully with sobering up the individual who has been on a drinking spree. A man in his forties had been drinking from December 27 to January 10. He was paralyzed drunk when seen. He was given six teaspoonfuls of honey. Twenty minutes later he was given another six teaspoonfuls, and twenty minutes later a third dose in the same amount. This made 18 teaspoonfuls of honey in 40 minutes. Beside his bed was a fifth of liquor, with one drink left in the bottle. Three hours later the drink was still there. Treatment was continued: three doses of six teaspoonfuls of honey each, repeated at 20-minute intervals.

The following morning he was seen at 8:30. He had slept straight through the night until 7:30 A.M. This was something he had not experienced for 20 years. He had, however, taken the one remaining drink of liquor. First he was given three doses of six teaspoonfuls of honey at intervals of 20 minutes. He was then given a soft-boiled egg. Ten minutes later he received six teaspoonfuls of honey. His lunch consisted of four teaspoonfuls of honey at the beginning of the meal, a glass of tomato juice, and a piece of ground beef. For dessert he received four more teaspoonfuls of honey.

A friend brought him a pint of liquor which was placed on the table with his evening meal. He pushed it away, and said he did not want it any more. He never took another drink.

GET THIS **NATURAL REMEDY BIBLE**

Worth 16^{95} ... FOR ONLY

5^{95}

**AUTHENTIC,
COMPLETE AND
UNALTERED EDITION
... JUST OFF THE PRESS**

SAVE $11.00

**704 Pages—Packed With
The FACTS You Want
To Know!**

THE ORIGINAL
Back To Eden

By Jethro Kloss

A HUMAN INTEREST STORY OF HEALTH ......

Answers questions for you that have never been answered before. Stop eating food that makes you sick! Discover which living habits are robbing you and your family of precious life and health, energy, endurance, beauty and the sheer vitality that brings joy to living. A fascinating "how to" classic that may well dispel your worries and anxieties, and save you many dollars as you apply the simple self-help clearly explained in this Bible of natural remedy books.

Millions of copies sold for up to $16.95! Now you can receive your copy at this Special Low Price of $5.95. Don't Delay! Ask for the Original Unaltered Edition of **Back To Eden** from your local bookstore or health food shop. If you cannot find the book, you may order directly from the publisher:

B. Lust

Health Products
& Services Since 1896

BENEDICT LUST PUBLICATIONS

P.O. Box 404 • New York, New York 10156

For Complete Catalog

of Natural Health Literature

send $1.00 to

BENEDICT LUST PUBLICATIONS

The Original Health Book People

P.O. Box 404

New York, N.Y. 10156-0404